I0824582

LETHAL STRIKERS

SAW-SCALED VIPER

AFRICA'S DEADLY SNAKE

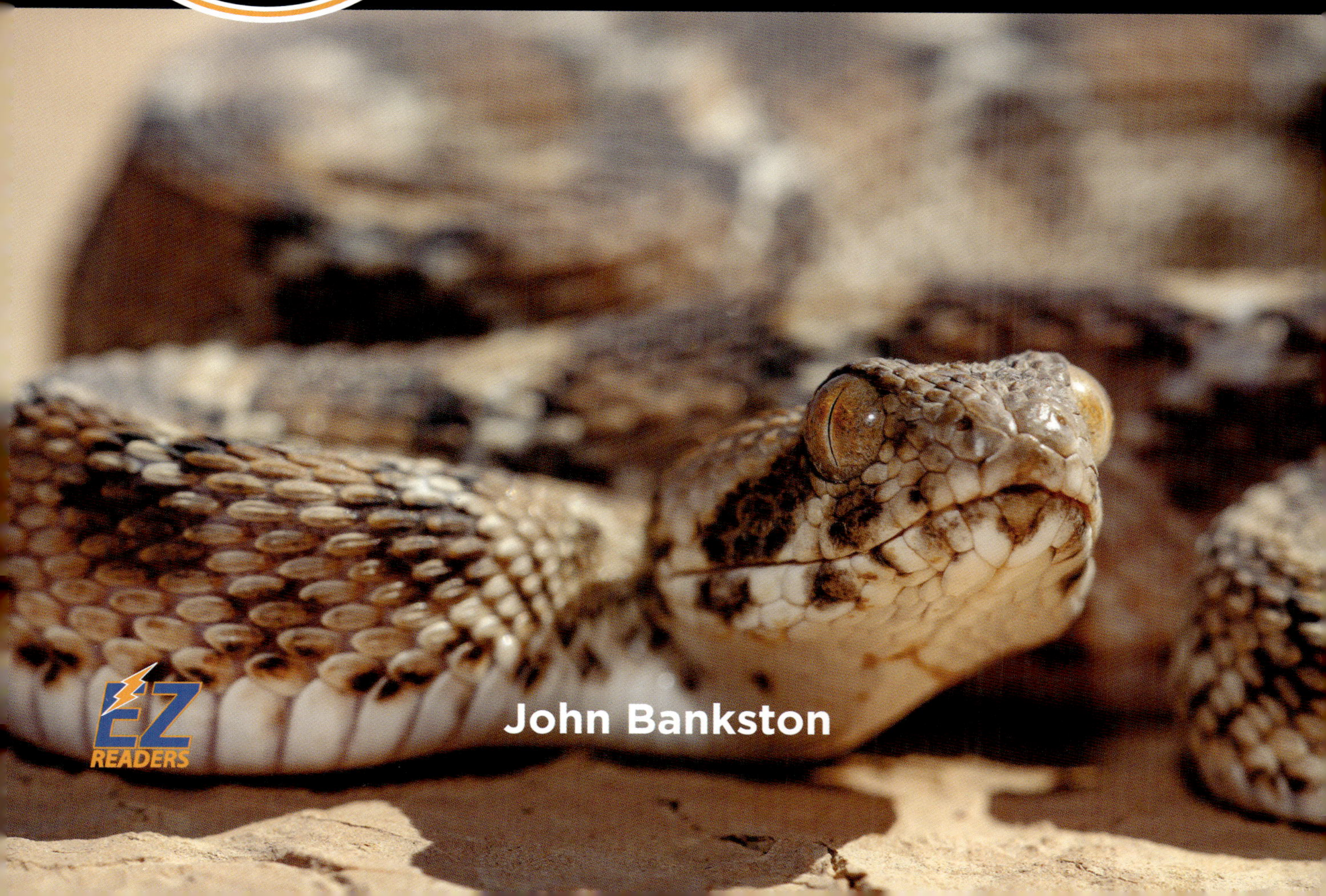

John Bankston

EZ READERS

Creating Young Nonfiction Readers

EZ Readers lets children delve into nonfiction at beginning reading levels. Young readers are introduced to new concepts, facts, ideas, and vocabulary.

Tips for Reading Nonfiction with Beginning Readers

Talk about Nonfiction
Begin by explaining that nonfiction books give us information that is true. The book will be organized around a specific topic or idea, and we may learn new facts through reading.

Look at the Parts
Most nonfiction books have helpful features. Our *EZ Readers* include a Contents page, an index, and color photographs. Share the purpose of these features with your reader.

Contents
Located at the front of a book, the Contents displays a list of the big ideas within the book and where to find them.

Index
An index is an alphabetical list of topics and the page numbers where they are found.

Photos/Charts
A lot of information can be found by "reading" the charts and photos found within nonfiction text. Help your reader learn more about the different ways information can be displayed.

With a little help and guidance about reading nonfiction, you can feel good about introducing a young reader to the world of *EZ Readers* nonfiction books.

Mitchell Lane

PUBLISHERS

2001 SW 31st Avenue
Hallandale, FL 33009
www.mitchelllane.com

First Edition, 2023.

Author: John Bankston
Designer: Ed Morgan
Editor: Morgan Brody

Title: Saw-Scaled Viper: Africa's Deadly Snake
Description: Hallandale, FL : Mitchell Lane Publishers, [2023]

Series: Lethal Strikers: Africa's Deadliest Snakes
Library bound ISBN: 978-1-68020-776-7
eBook ISBN: 978-1-68020-777-4

EZ Readers is an imprint of Mitchell Lane Publishers.

Photo credits: Shutterstock

CONTENTS

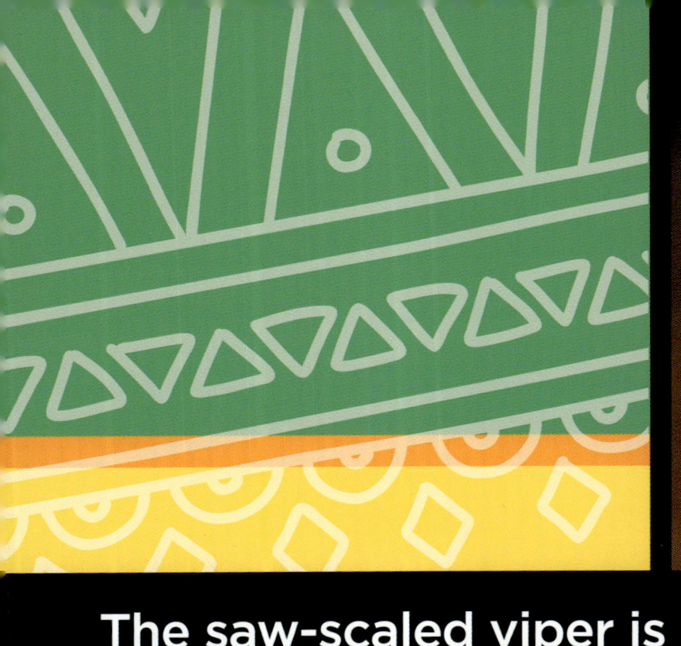

The saw-scaled viper is a tiny snake with a highly **venomous** bite. It spends the day in empty **burrows** or hidden beneath rocks. As the sun sets, this fierce hunter emerges to feed.

This two-foot long snake is **nocturnal**. It's also an **ambush predator**. Most predators chase their food. The saw-scaled viper just waits for it. After a rainfall, these snakes slither out by the dozens. Groups hang from trees or cluster near rocks.

Saw-scaled vipers succeed by living in places most snakes avoid. They don't mind cities. They do well in very dry **environments** like the Middle East.

Like other ambush predators, their colors help them disappear. Some saw-scaled vipers are red with zigzag stripes. Others are orange, brown, or gray with darker splotches and spots. These colors create **camouflage**.

As reptiles, most snakes lay eggs. However, female saw-scaled vipers' eggs hatch inside their bodies. They usually have over 20 babies. The small snakes take care of themselves. Saw-scaled vipers can live for over 20 years.

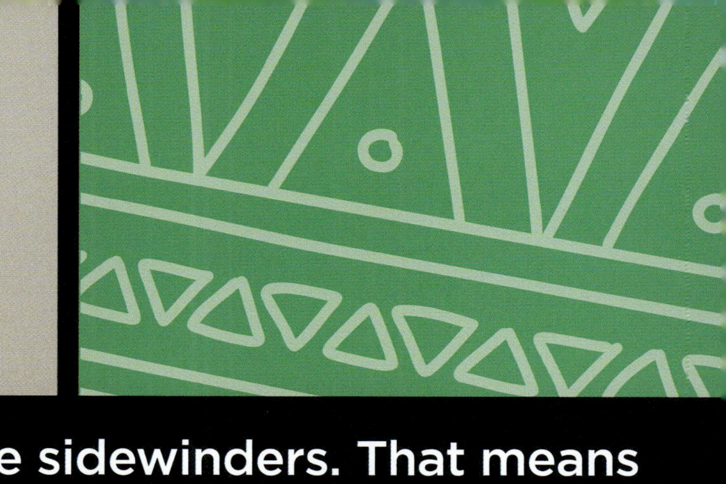

These vipers are sidewinders. That means when they move most of their body is off the ground. Folding into an S-shape, they slither sideways—like rattlesnakes. The saw-scaled viper barely touches the surface. That makes it perfect for really hot, sandy places!

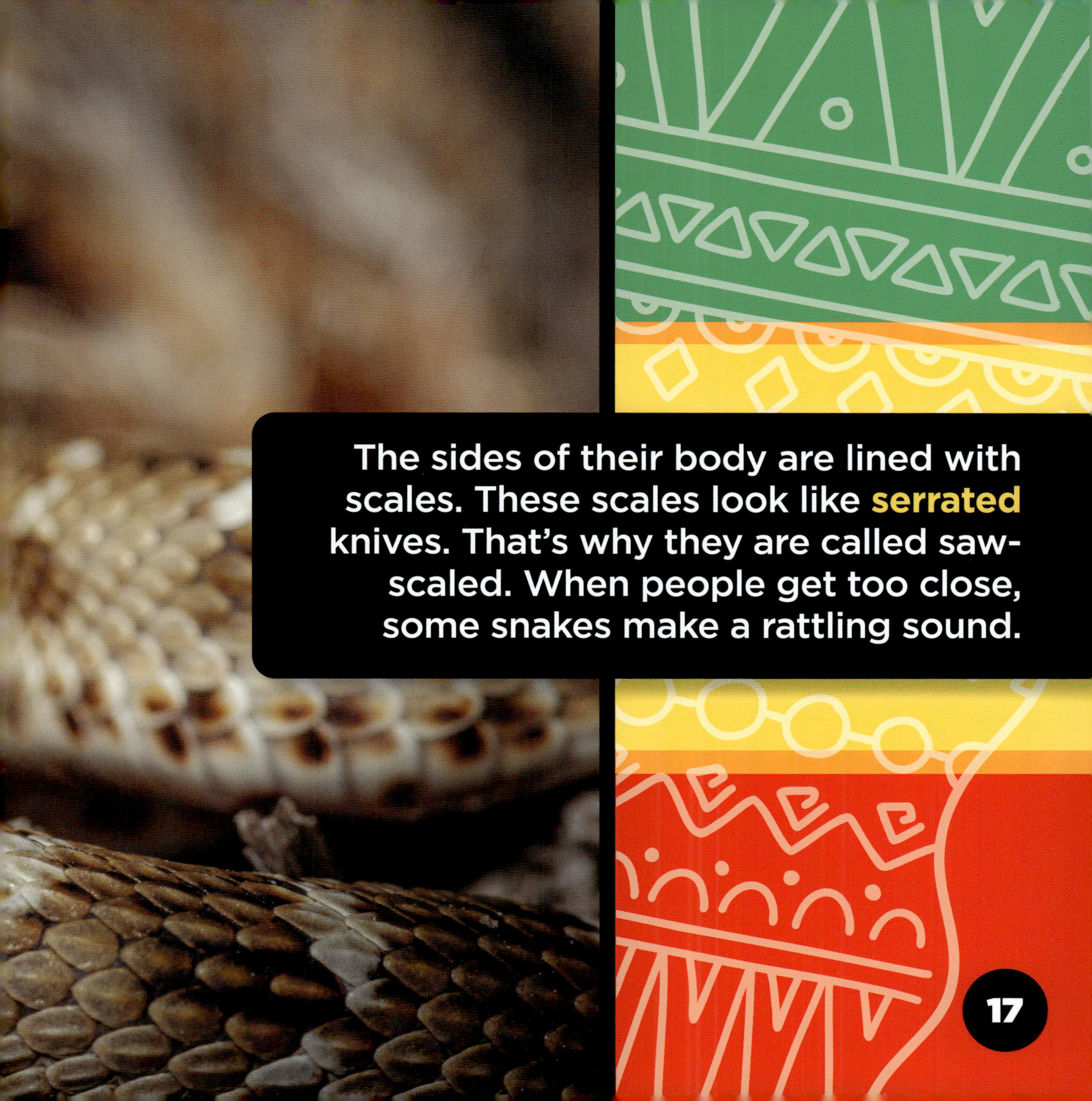

The sides of their body are lined with scales. These scales look like **serrated** knives. That's why they are called saw-scaled. When people get too close, some snakes make a rattling sound.

Others hiss. When these snakes rub their saw scales together, it sounds like bacon sizzling in a pan or a boiling tea kettle. If you hear a sound like that and you're not in a kitchen, it's a good idea to slowly back away.

How do Saw-Scaled Vipers KILL?

The toad never sees the saw-scaled viper coming. The saw-scaled viper is just inches away. It's perfectly hidden by the shadows of a rock. Its head and upper body dart out so quickly it's just a blur. The bite happens in less than a second. **Venom** kills the toad almost instantly. The viper keeps waiting—waiting for the toad to die. When that happens, the saw-scaled viper opens its mouth extra wide and swallows its supper whole.

Where Do **Saw-Scaled Vipers** Live?

They are mainly found in the Middle East, which includes Egypt, Libya, the Sudan, and Saudi Arabia. They are also found in parts of Western Africa.

Interesting **Facts**

- A saw-scaled viper's bite releases enough **venom** to kill six people.
- Anti-venom for saw-scaled snakes in India doesn't work with African saw-scaled snakes because they are different **species**.
- Wherever there are saw-scaled vipers, they kill more people than all other snakes combined.
- They have highly lethal venom that causes most victims to die before they ever reach a hospital.
- Although thousands die from saw-scaled bites every year, the snakes also help people. That's because their venom is used in medicine.

Parts of a Saw-Scaled Viper

Head
The head is wider than the neck and shaped like a pear. Their fangs fold into their mouth.

Eyes
The large yellow eyes have vertically slit **pupils**.

Body
Their body is short and thick and their tail is short and thin. The body is lined with serrated scales. They may also have many orange or dark brown spots on their bodies.

Glossary

ambush predator
A meat-eating animal that captures its target secretly rather than by speed or strength

burrow
A hole dug by a small animal like a rabbit

camouflage
Colors that let animals blend into their surroundings

environment
Type of conditions where an animal lives

nocturnal
Active at night

pupil
The circular opening at the center of the iris in the eye

serrated
A knife with a jagged or saw-like edge

species
Very similar animals that can breed

venom
Poison used by an animal

venomous
Animal with venom

Further Reading

Fly Guy Presents: Snakes. NY: Scholastic. 2016.

Hansen, Grace. *Snakes*. North Mankato, MN: Capstone. 2016.

Hirschmann, Kris. *Top Ten Deadly Snakes: Go Face to Fang with the World's 10 Deadliest Snakes*. 2020.

Simon, Seymour. *Poisonous Snakes.* Mineola, NY: Dover. 2012.

Starkey, Michael G. *Snakes for Kids: A Junior Scientist's Guide to Venom, Scales, and Life in the Wild.* Emeryville, CA: Rockridge Press. 2020.

On the Internet

Find out more about the the saw-scaled viper from Kidadl:
https://kidadl.com/facts/animals/saw-scaled-viper-facts

There's also a page you can color:
https://kidadl.com/free-coloring-pages/saw-scaled-viper

Mark's Reptiles has some helpful info:
https://www.youtube.com/watch?v=R_y3De7jhz4

Listen to the sound made by a saw-scaled snake on BBC's Earth Unplugged:
https://www.youtube.com/watch?v=RUG2fK1-ATg

Index